For Aunt Bev and Tracy

authortinabiby.pubsitepro.com

ISBN 979-8-218-42540-1 (paperback)

All rights reserved. No part of this publication may be reproduced, distributed, or transmitted in any form or by any means, including photocopying, recording or other electronic or mechanical methods without the prior written permission of the publisher and author. For permission requests, solicit the author via the email below.

authortinabiby@gmail.com

Printed in the United States of America

Copyright (c) 2024 by Tina Biby

On a warm, spring day, Marie and Diane were walking to their Aunt Sue's house to help her make jelly.

When the girls arrived at Aunt Sue's house, she was in the back yard feeding her chickens.

The girls wondered why they were walking up the hill behind Aunt Sue's farm. Marie asked, "What are we doing, Aunt Sue?" "Ya," asked Diane, "I thought we were making jelly today?" Aunt Sue smiled and said, "You'll see."

"What are we doing here, Aunt Sue?" Asked Marie.
"I don't see any berries up here." Said Diane.
Aunt Sue said, "We aren't picking berries, girls."
"Well, then what are we picking to make
the jelly?" Asked Diane.

Aunt Sue replied, "Look around you, girls."
"What do you see?"
"Yellow Flowers," Answered Diane.
"Ya, lots of them." said Marie.
"Those are called dandelions." Replied Aunt Sue.
"They are pretty, but why are we here?" asked Diane.
Aunt Sue told the girls they were picking the dandelions to make the jelly.
The girls were surprised.
"I didn't know we could eat dandelions!" Exclaimed Diane.

As the girls began filling their baskets, Aunt Sue continued to tell them about dandelions. "My grandma's family made dandelion jelly for many generations, and we can eat the blossoms and stems in salad."
"Dandelions are free food growing all around us, and they are very good for us too!"

Marie asked Aunt Sue, 'How are they good for us?"
"I thought they were a weed or wild flower," Said Diane.
"They are," Said Aunt Sue, "But, they are very good for us."
"My grandpa ground the dandelion root and
made coffee."
"Did he drink that?" Asked Marie
"Yes, he did, Marie," Said Aunt Sue.
"Yuck!" Said Diane, "I don't like coffee."

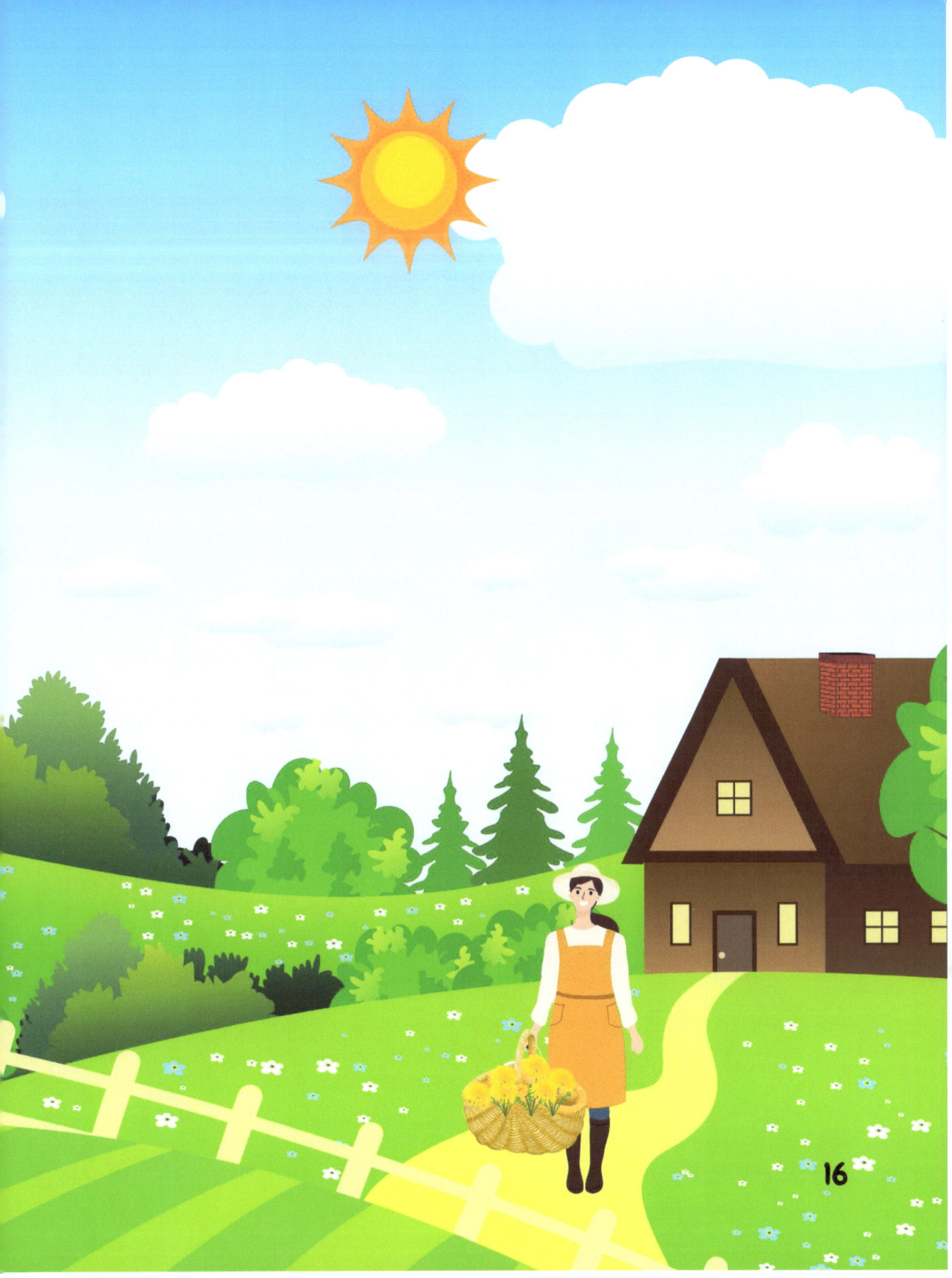

Marie asked, "How do we make jelly from these dandelions, Aunt Sue?"

The girls were curious and excited to learn how to make dandelion jelly. "First," instructed Aunt Sue, "We rinse the blossoms gently, in cool water."
"Why gently?" Asked Diane.
"So we do not rinse off too much nectar," replied Aunt Sue.

"What is nectar?" Asked Marie.
"Nectar is a food source for bees and other insects." Replied Aunt Sue.
Marie Said, "Oh, that's why we see so many bees in spring."
"Ya, they are hungry after the long winter." Diane said.

"That is correct," Said Aunt Sue, "And, they are good for us too!"
"How are they good for us?" Asked Diane
"They provide us with lots of vitamins and minerals." Replied Aunt Sue.
"Wow!" exclaimed Diane.
"They are really good for us."

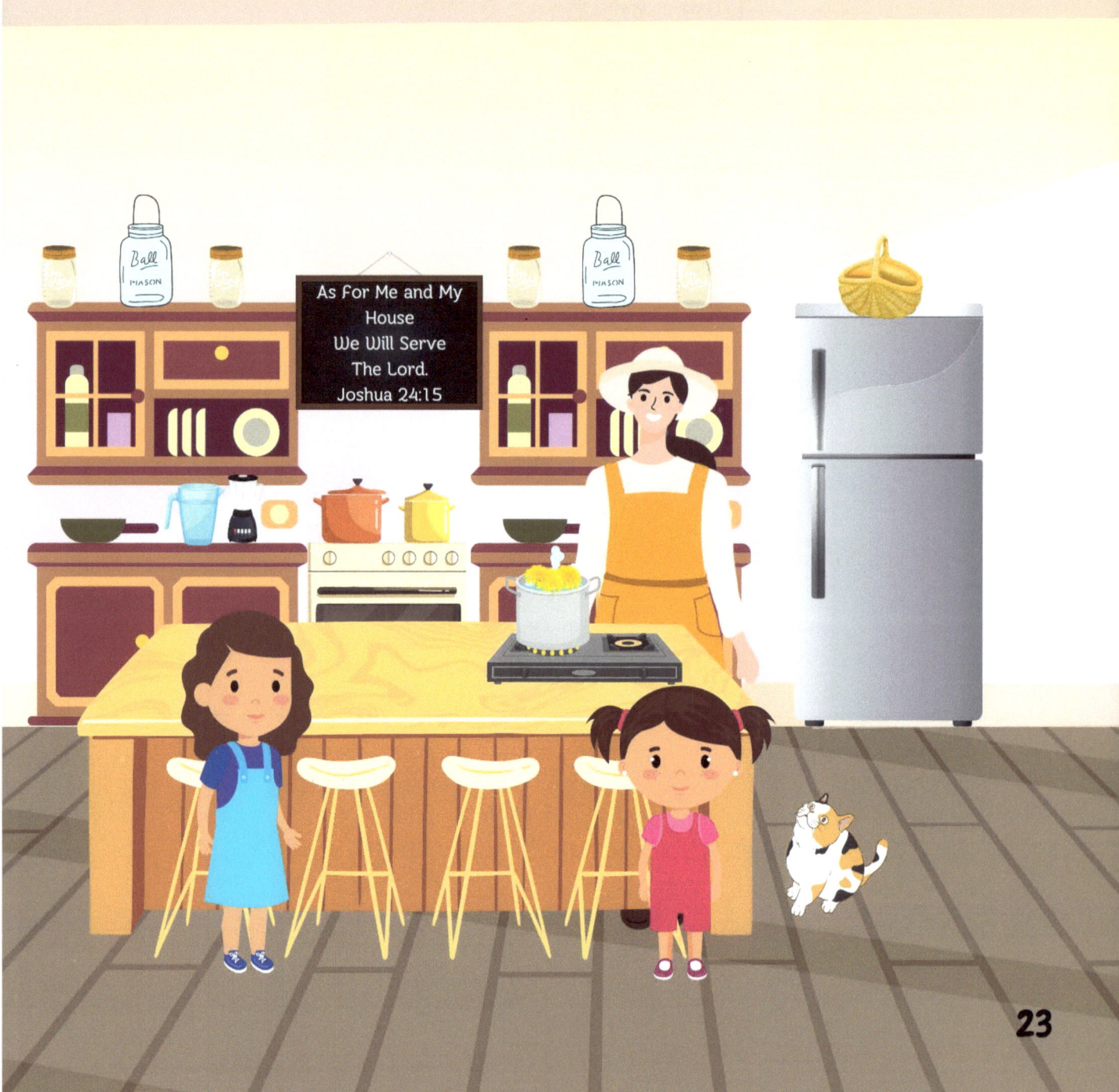

"What do we do next, Aunt Sue?" Asked Marie. Aunt Sue Replied, "Next, we boil the dandelion blossoms for 3 minutes to extract the nectar, to make the dandelion juice."

"Now, we strain the blossoms from the juice and pour it into a cook pot to boil." Instructed Aunt Sue.
"Next, we add the lemon juice, and pectin."
"What is pectin?" Asked Marie.
Aunt Sue explained to the girls that Pectin is found in fruit and is used to thicken the jelly.

"What do we do next, Aunt Sue?" Asked Marie.
Aunt Sue asked the girls to help her
add the sugar to the dandelion juice.
The girls sat on stools behind the counter
so they could help pour the sugar
into the hot, bubbly, dandelion juice.

The girls walked over to the kitchen table, and sat on the chairs, and watched as Aunt Sue began to pour the hot, dandelion juice into the jars. The girls helped Aunt Sue put the lids onto the jars.

A few minutes later, the jars began to make popping sounds.
Aunt Sue told the girls they make popping sounds as the jars begin to seal. She said, "When our jelly jars cool and seal, we can store it in the pantry for a couple years."
"That means we can eat jelly all winter long!" Said Marie.
"The longer the jelly sits, the better it tastes, too." Said Aunt Sue.

Aunt Sue opened one of the jars of dandelion jelly for the girls to try. Diane said, "This tastes like honey!"
"Ya, it's yummy, too!" Agreed Marie
Aunt Sue thanked the girls for helping.
Both girls agreed they had fun picking dandelions and helping Aunt Sue.

The girls enjoyed learning how to make dandelion jelly. But, most of all, they enjoyed spending the day with their Aunt Sue.

THANK YOU SO MUCH

Thank you for reading and sharing my book with your loved ones.

I have been writing and publishing children's books since 2017, and I am still amazed by the inspiration and ideas I receive daily by the children I work with and those around me.

My journey began in 2017 when I wrote my first unpublished book about hatching chicken eggs for a local preschool.

I read my unpublished version to the class. After reading the book, the teachers in the classroom encouraged me to publish my book.

In 2018, I published my first book. "Special Eggs: Where Do They Come From?"

I published other books since then.

And continue to write and publish to this day.

Thank you again, for reading my books!

Please write a review on Amazon and share.

God Bless,

TINA BIBY

authortinabiby.pubsitepro.com

Dandelion Jelly

By Beverly Walters
(Author Tina Biby's Aunt)

What you will need:
1 Quart of Dandelion Blossoms
1 Quart of Water
1 Package of Pectin
2 Tablespoons of Lemon Juice
4-1/2 Cups of Sugar
Yellow Food Coloring (Optional)

Rinse the blossoms in cool water, carefully. Boil them for 3 minutes in the water, strain, and return to the stove to and add lemon juice and pectin. When this begins to boil, add sugar and boil 3 minutes more. Add the food coloring and pour into prepared jars and seal.

This jelly tastes like honey!

www.ingramcontent.com/pod-product-compliance
Lightning Source LLC
LaVergne TN
LVHW070441070526
838199LV00036B/674